THE LITTLE LIBRARY OF
EARTH MEDICINE

BROWN BEAR

Kenneth Meadows

Illustrations by Jo Donegan

DK PUBLISHING, INC.

A DK PUBLISHING BOOK

The Little Library of Earth Medicine was
produced, edited, and designed by
GLS Editorial and Design
Garden Studios, 11-15 Betterton Street
London WC2H 9BP

Editorial director: Jane Laing
Design director: Ruth Shane
Project designer: Luke Herriott
Editors: Claire Calman, Terry Burrows, Victoria Sorzano
US Editors: Jennifer Dorr, William Lach, Barbara Minton

Additional illustrations: Roy Flooks 16, 17, 31; John Lawrence 38
Special photography: Mark Hamilton
Picture credits: American Natural History Museum 8-9, 12, 14-15; San Diego Museum of Man
(photograph by John Oldenkamp) 32

First American Edition, 1998
2 4 6 8 10 9 7 5 3 1

Published in the United States by DK Publishing, Inc.
95 Madison Avenue, New York, NY 10016
Visit us on the World Wide Web at http://www.dk.com.

Library of Congress Cataloging-in-Publication Data
Meadows, Kenneth.
    The little library of earth medicine / by Kenneth Meadows. – 1st American ed.
        p   cm.
    Contents: |1| Falcon, 21st March-19th April – |2| Beaver, 20th April-20 May – |3|
Deer, 21st May-20th June – |4| Woodpecker, 21st June-21st July – |5| Salmon, 22nd July-
21st August – |6| Brown Bear, 22nd August-21st September – |7| Crow, 22nd
September-22nd October – |8| Snake, 23rd October-22nd November – |9| Owl, 23rd
November-21st December – |10| Goose, 22nd December-19 January – |11| Otter, 20th
January-18th February – |12| Wolf, 19th February-20th March
    Includes indexes.
    ISBN 0-7894-2877-6
    1. Medicine wheels–Miscellanea. 2. Horoscopes. 3. Indians of North
America–Religion–Miscellanea. 4. Typology (Psychology)–Miscellanea. I. Title.
BF1623.M43M42 1998
133.5'9397–dc21   97-42267
                                                                                              CIP

Reproduced by Kestrel Digital Colour Ltd, Chelmsford, Essex
Printed and bound in Hong Kong by Imago

CONTENTS

INTRODUCING
EARTH MEDICINE

To Native Americans, medicine is not an external substance but an inner power that is found in both nature and ourselves.

Earth Medicine is a unique method of personality profiling that draws on Native American understanding of the Universe, and on the principles embodied in sacred Medicine Wheels.

Native Americans believed that spirit, although invisible, permeated Nature, so that everything in Nature was sacred. Animals were perceived as acting as

Shaman's rattle
Shamans used rattles to connect with their inner spirit. This is a Tlingit shaman's wooden rattle.

messengers of spirit. They also appeared in waking dreams to impart power known as "medicine." The recipients of such dreams honored the animal species that appeared to them by rendering their images on ceremonial, ornamental, and everyday artifacts.

NATURE WITHIN SELF
Native American shamans – tribal wisemen – recognized similarities between the natural forces prevalent during the seasons and the characteristics of those born

"Spirit has provided you with an opportunity to study in Nature's university." Stoney teaching

during corresponding times of the year. They also noted how personality is affected by the four phases of the Moon – at birth and throughout life – and by the continual alternation of energy flow, from active to passive. This view is encapsulated in Earth Medicine, which helps you to recognize how the dynamics of Nature function within you and how the potential strengths you were born with can be developed.

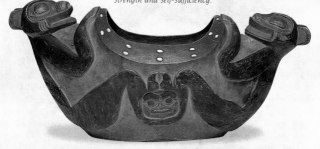

Animal ornament
To the Anasazi, who carved this ornament from jet, the frog symbolized adaptability.

MEDICINE WHEELS

Native American cultural traditions embrace a variety of circular symbolic images and objects. These sacred hoops have become known as Medicine

Feast dish
Stylized bear carvings adorn this Tlingit feast dish. To the Native American, the bear symbolizes strength and self-sufficiency.

Wheels, due to their similarity to the spoked wheels of the wagons that carried settlers into the heartlands of once-Native American territory. Each Medicine Wheel showed how different objects or qualities related to one another within the context of a greater whole, and how different forces and energies moved within it.

One Medicine Wheel might be regarded as the master wheel because it indicated balance within Nature and the most effective way of achieving harmony with the Universe and ourselves. It is upon this master Medicine Wheel (see pp.10–11) that Earth Medicine is structured.

THE MEDICINE WHEEL

The outer Wheel is divided into twelve birth times, each of which has its own animal totem, and stone, tree, and color affinities. At the hub of the Wheel, surrounded by representations of Elements, Directions, and energy flow, is the Wakan-Tanka – symbol of invisible energies coming into physical reality.

Season of birth
Each of the twelve segments relates to a specific time of year (see pp.12–13).

Wakan-Tanka
The powerful symbol used by some Native Americans to denote energy coming into form (see p.24).

NORTH: WINTER

WEST: AUTUMN

WOLF

OTTER

GOOSE

OWL

SNAKE

CROW

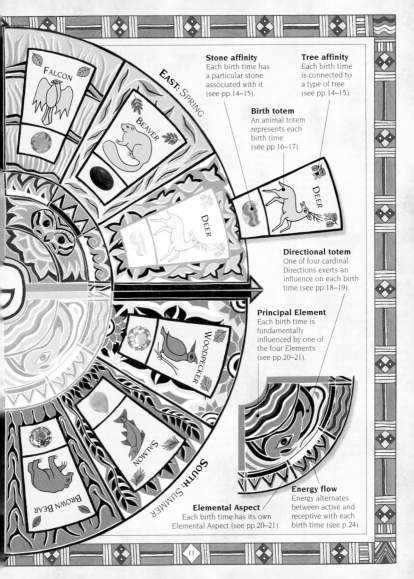

Stone affinity
Each birth time has a particular stone associated with it (see pp.14–15).

Tree affinity
Each birth time is connected to a type of tree (see pp.14–15).

Birth totem
An animal totem represents each birth time (see pp.16–17).

Directional totem
One of four cardinal Directions exerts an influence on each birth time (see pp.18–19).

Principal Element
Each birth time is fundamentally influenced by one of the four Elements (see pp.20–21).

Energy flow
Energy alternates between active and receptive with each birth time (see p.24).

Elemental Aspect
Each birth time has its own Elemental Aspect (see pp.20–21).

EAST: SPRING

FALCON

BEAVER

DEER

DEER

WOODPECKER

SALMON

BROWN BEAR

SOUTH: SUMMER

THE TWELVE
BIRTH TIMES

THE STRUCTURE OF THE MEDICINE WHEEL IS BASED
UPON THE SEASONS TO REFLECT THE POWERFUL
INFLUENCE OF NATURE ON HUMAN PERSONALITY.

he Medicine Wheel classifies human nature into twelve personality types, each corresponding to the characteristics of Nature at a particular time of the year. It is designed to act as a kind of map to help you discover your strengths and weaknesses, your inner drives and instinctive behaviors, and your true potential.

The four seasons form the basis of the Wheel's structure, with the Summer and Winter solstices and the Spring and Autumn equinoxes marking each season's passing. In Earth Medicine,

each season is a metaphor for a stage of human growth and development. Spring is likened to infancy and the newness of life, and Summer to the exuberance of youth and of rapid development. Autumn represents the fulfillment that mature adulthood brings, while Winter symbolizes the accumulated wisdom that can be drawn upon in later life.

Each seasonal quarter of the Wheel is further divided into three periods, making twelve time segments altogether. The time of your birth determines the direction from which

Seasonal rites

Performers at the Iroquois mid-Winter ceremony wore masks made of braided maize husks. They danced to attune themselves to energies that would ensure a good harvest.

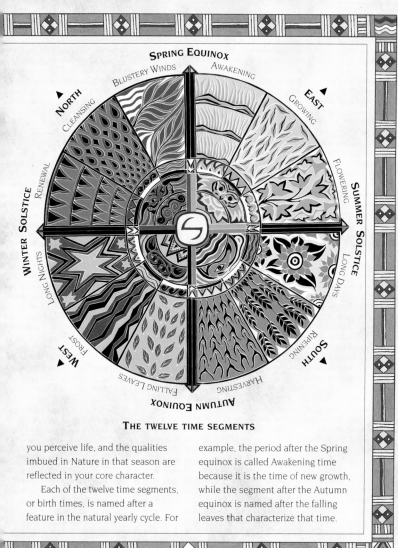

THE TWELVE TIME SEGMENTS

you perceive life, and the qualities imbued in Nature in that season are reflected in your core character.

Each of the twelve time segments, or birth times, is named after a feature in the natural yearly cycle. For example, the period after the Spring equinox is called Awakening time because it is the time of new growth, while the segment after the Autumn equinox is named after the falling leaves that characterize that time.

THE SIGNIFICANCE OF
TOTEMS

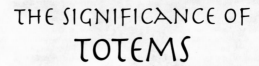

NATIVE AMERICANS BELIEVED THAT TOTEMS — ANIMAL SYMBOLS — REPRESENTED ESSENTIAL TRUTHS AND ACTED AS CONNECTIONS TO NATURAL POWERS.

A totem is an animal or natural object adopted as an emblem to typify certain distinctive qualities. Native Americans regarded animals, whose behavior is predictable, as particularly useful guides to categorizing human patterns of behavior.

A totem mirrors aspects of your nature and unlocks the intuitive knowledge that lies beyond the reasoning capacity of the intellect. It may take the form of a carving or molding, a pictorial image, or a token of fur, feather, bone, tooth, or claw. Its presence serves as an immediate link with the energies it represents. A totem is therefore more effective than a glyph or symbol as an aid to comprehending nonphysical powers and formative forces.

PRIMARY TOTEMS

In Earth Medicine you have three primary totems: a birth totem, a Directional totem, and an Elemental totem. Your *birth totem* is the embodiment of core characteristics that correspond with the dominant aspects of Nature during your birth time.

Symbol of strength
The handle of this Tlingit knife is carved with a raven and a bear head, symbols of insight and inner strength.

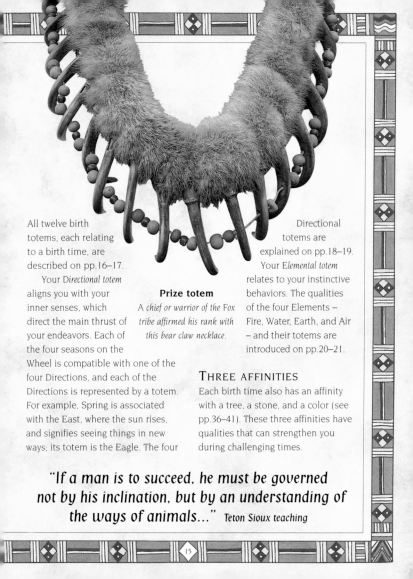

All twelve birth totems, each relating to a birth time, are described on pp.16–17.

Your *Directional totem* aligns you with your inner senses, which direct the main thrust of your endeavors. Each of the four seasons on the Wheel is compatible with one of the four Directions, and each of the Directions is represented by a totem. For example, Spring is associated with the East, where the sun rises, and signifies seeing things in new ways; its totem is the Eagle. The four

Prize totem

A chief or warrior of the Fox tribe affirmed his rank with this bear claw necklace.

Directional totems are explained on pp.18–19. Your *Elemental totem* relates to your instinctive behaviors. The qualities of the four Elements – Fire, Water, Earth, and Air – and their totems are introduced on pp.20–21.

THREE AFFINITIES

Each birth time also has an affinity with a tree, a stone, and a color (see pp.36–41). These three affinities have qualities that can strengthen you during challenging times.

"If a man is to succeed, he must be governed not by his inclination, but by an understanding of the ways of animals..." *Teton Sioux teaching*

THE TWELVE
BIRTH TOTEMS

THE TWELVE BIRTH TIMES ARE REPRESENTED BY TOTEMS,
EACH ONE AN ANIMAL THAT BEST EXPRESSES THE
QUALITIES INHERENT IN THAT BIRTH TIME.

Earth Medicine associates an animal totem with each birth time (the two sets of dates below reflect the difference in season between the Northern and Southern Hemispheres). These animals help to connect you to the powers and abilities that they represent. For an in-depth study of the Brown Bear birth totem, see pp.28–29.

FALCON
March 21 – April 19 (N. Hem)
Sept 22 – Oct 22 (S. Hem)
Falcons are full of initiative, but often rush in to make decisions they may later regret. Lively and extroverted, they have enthusiasm for new experiences but can sometimes lack persistence.

DEER
May 21 – June 20 (N. Hem)
Nov 23 – Dec 21 (S. Hem)
Deer are willing to sacrifice the old for the new. They loathe routine, thriving on variety and challenges. They have a wild side, often leaping from one situation or relationship into another without reflection.

BEAVER
April 20 – May 20 (N. Hem)
Oct 23 – Nov 22 (S. Hem)
Practical and steady, Beavers have a capacity for perseverance. Good homemakers, they are warm and affectionate but need harmony and peace to avoid becoming irritable. They have a keen aesthetic sense.

WOODPECKER
June 21 – July 21 (N. Hem)
Dec 22 – Jan 19 (S. Hem)
Emotional and sensitive, Woodpeckers are warm to those closest to them, and willing to sacrifice their needs for those of their loved ones. They have lively imaginations but can be worriers.

SALMON
July 22 – August 21 (N. Hem)
Jan 20 – Feb 18 (S. Hem)
Enthusiastic and self-confident, Salmon people enjoy running things. They are uncompromising and forceful, and can occasionally seem a little arrogant or self-important. They are easily hurt by neglect.

BROWN BEAR
August 22 – Sept 21 (N. Hem)
Feb 19 – March 20 (S. Hem)
Brown Bears are hardworking, practical, and self-reliant. They do not like change, preferring to stick to what is familiar. They have a flair for fixing things, are good-natured, and make good friends.

CROW
Sept 22 – Oct 22 (N. Hem)
March 21 – April 19 (S. Hem)
Crows dislike solitude and feel most comfortable in company. Although usually pleasant and good-natured, they can be strongly influenced by negative atmospheres, becoming gloomy and prickly.

SNAKE
Oct 23 – Nov 22 (N. Hem)
April 20 – May 20 (S. Hem)
Snakes are secretive and mysterious, hiding their feelings beneath a cool exterior. Adaptable, determined, and imaginative, they are capable of bouncing back from tough situations encountered in life.

OWL
Nov 23 – Dec 21 (N. Hem)
May 21 – June 20 (S. Hem)
Owls need freedom of expression. They are lively, self-reliant, and have an eye for detail. Inquisitive and adaptable, they have a tendency to overextend themselves. Owls are often physically courageous.

GOOSE
Dec 22 – Jan 19 (N. Hem)
June 21 – July 21 (S. Hem)
Goose people are far-sighted idealists who are willing to explore the unknown. They approach life with enthusiasm, determined to fulfill their dreams. They are perfectionists, and can appear unduly serious.

OTTER
Jan 20 – Feb 18 (N. Hem)
July 22 – August 21 (S. Hem)
Otters are friendly, lively, and perceptive. They feel inhibited by too many rules and regulations, which often makes them appear eccentric. They like cleanliness and order, and have original minds.

WOLF
Feb 19 – March 20 (N. Hem)
August 22 – Sept 21 (S. Hem)
Wolves are sensitive, artistic, and intuitive – people to whom others turn for help. They value freedom and their own space, and are easily affected by others. They are philosophical, trusting, and genuine.

THE INFLUENCE OF THE
DIRECTIONS

ALSO KNOWN BY NATIVE AMERICANS AS THE FOUR
WINDS, THE INFLUENCE OF THE FOUR DIRECTIONS IS
EXPERIENCED THROUGH YOUR INNER SENSES.

R egarded as the "keepers" or "caretakers" of the Universe, the four Directions or alignments were also referred to by Native Americans as the four Winds because their presence was felt rather than seen.

DIRECTIONAL TOTEMS
In Earth Medicine, each Direction or Wind is associated with a season and a time of day. Thus the Summer birth times – Long Days time, Ripening time, and Harvesting time – all

fall within the South Direction, and afternoon. The Direction to which your birth time belongs influences the nature of your inner senses.

The East Direction is associated with illumination. Its totem is the Eagle – a bird that soars closest to the Sun and can see clearly from height. The South is the Direction of Summer and the afternoon. It signifies growth and fruition, fluidity, and emotions. Its totem, the Mouse, symbolizes productivity, feelings, and an ability to perceive detail.

"Remember...the circle of the sky, the stars, the supernatural Winds breathing night and day...the four Directions." Pawnee teaching

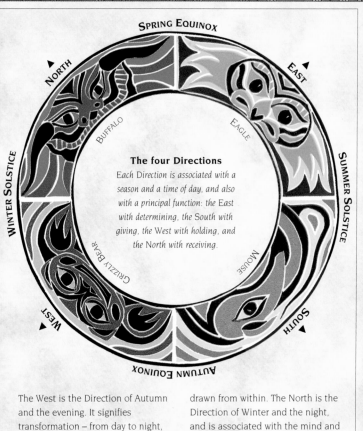

The four Directions

Each Direction is associated with a season and a time of day, and also with a principal function: the East with determining, the South with giving, the West with holding, and the North with receiving.

SPRING EQUINOX

NORTH

EAST

BUFFALO

EAGLE

WINTER SOLSTICE

SUMMER SOLSTICE

GRIZZLY BEAR

MOUSE

WEST

SOUTH

AUTUMN EQUINOX

The West is the Direction of Autumn and the evening. It signifies transformation – from day to night, from Summer to Winter – and the qualities of introspection and conservation. Its totem is the Grizzly Bear, which represents strength drawn from within. The North is the Direction of Winter and the night, and is associated with the mind and its sustenance – knowledge. Its totem is the Buffalo, an animal that was honored by Native Americans as the great material "provider."

THE INFLUENCE OF THE
ELEMENTS

THE FOUR ELEMENTS – AIR, FIRE, WATER, AND EARTH –
PERVADE EVERYTHING AND INDICATE THE NATURE OF
MOVEMENT AND THE ESSENCE OF WHO YOU ARE.

E lements are intangible qualities that describe the essential state or character of all things. In Earth Medicine, the four Elements are allied with four fundamental modes of activity and are associated with different aspects of the self. Air expresses free movement in all directions; it is related to the mind and to thinking. Fire indicates expansive motion; it is linked with the spirit and with intuition. Water signifies fluidity; it

Elemental profile
Brown Bear's configura-
tion is Earth of Water.
Water is the Principal
Element and Earth the
Elemental Aspect.

EARTH

FIRE

WATER

WATER

FIRE

AIR

has associations with the soul and the emotions. Earth symbolizes stability; it is related to the physical body and the sensations.

ELEMENTAL DISTRIBUTION

On the Medicine Wheel one Element is associated with each of the four Directions – Fire in the East, Earth in the West, Air in the North, and Water in the South. These are known as the Principal Elements.

AIR

WATER

FIRE

EARTH

EARTH

AIR

The four Elements also have an individual association with each of the twelve birth times – known as the Elemental Aspects. They follow a cyclical sequence around the Wheel based on the action of the Sun (Fire) on the Earth, producing atmosphere (Air) and condensation (Water).

The three birth times that share an Elemental Aspect belong to the same Elemental family or "clan," with a totem that gives insight into its key qualities. Brown Bear people belong to the Turtle clan (see pp.34–35).

ELEMENTAL EMPHASIS

For each birth time, the qualities of the Elemental Aspect usually predominate over those of the Principal Element, although both are present to give a specific configuration, such as Fire of Earth (for Brown Bear's, see pp.34–35). For Falcon, Woodpecker, and Otter, the Principal Element and the Elemental Aspect are identical (for example, Air of Air), so people of these totems tend to express that Element intensely.

THE INFLUENCE OF THE MOON

THE WAXING AND WANING OF THE MOON DURING ITS FOUR PHASES HAS A CRUCIAL INFLUENCE ON THE FORMATION OF PERSONALITY AND HUMAN ENDEAVOR.

Native Americans regarded the Sun and Moon as indicators respectively of the active and receptive energies inherent in Nature (see p.24), as well as the measurers of time. They associated solar influences with conscious activity and the exercise of reason and the will, and lunar influences with subconscious activity and the emotional and intuitive aspects of human nature.

The Waxing Moon

This phase lasts for approximately eleven days. It is a time of growth and therefore ideal for developing new ideas and concentrating your efforts into new projects.

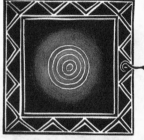

The Full Moon

Lasting about three days, this is when lunar power is at its height. It is therefore a good time for completing what was developed during the Waxing Moon.

THE FOUR PHASES

There are four phases in the twenty-nine-day lunar cycle, each one an expression of energy reflecting a particular mode of activity. They can be likened to the phases of growth of a flowering plant through the seasons: the emergence of buds (Waxing Moon), the bursting of flowers (Full Moon), the falling away of flowers (Waning Moon), and the germination of seeds (Dark Moon). The influence of each phase can be felt in two ways: in the formation of personality and in day-to-day life.

The energy expressed by the phase of the Moon at the time of your birth has a strong influence on personality. For instance, someone born during the Dark Moon is likely to be inward-looking, while a person born during the Full Moon may be more expressive. Someone born during a Waxing Moon is likely to have an outgoing nature, while a person born during a Waning Moon may be reserved. Consult a set of Moon tables to discover the phase the Moon was in on your birthday.

In your day-to-day life, the benefits of coming into harmony with the Moon's energies are considerable. Experience the energy of the four phases by consciously working with them. A Native American approach is described below.

The Waning Moon
A time for making changes, this phase lasts for an average of eleven days. Use it to improve and modify, and to dispose of what is no longer needed or wanted.

The Dark Moon
The Moon disappears from the sky for around four days. This is a time for contemplation of what has been achieved, and for germinating the seeds for the new.

THE INFLUENCE OF
ENERGY FLOW

THE MEDICINE WHEEL REFLECTS THE PERFECT
BALANCE OF THE COMPLEMENTARY ACTIVE AND
RECEPTIVE ENERGIES THAT COEXIST IN NATURE.

Energy flows through Nature in two complementary ways, which can be expressed in terms of active and receptive, or male and female. The active energy principle is linked with the Elements of Fire and Air, and the receptive principle with Water and Earth.

Each of the twelve birth times has an active or receptive energy related to its Elemental Aspect. Traveling around the Wheel, the two energies alternate with each birth time, resulting in an equal balance of active and receptive energies, as in Nature.

Active energy is associated with the Sun and conscious activity. Those whose birth times take this principle prefer to pursue experience. They are conceptual,

energetic, outgoing, practical, and analytical. Receptive energy is associated with the Moon and subconscious activity. Those whose birth times take this principle prefer to attract experience. They are intuitive, reflective, conserving, emotional, and nurturing.

THE WAKAN-TANKA

At the heart of the Wheel lies an S-shape within a circle, the symbol of the life-giving source of everything that comes into physical existence – seemingly out of nothing. Named by the Plains Indians as Wakan-Tanka (Great Power), it can also be perceived as energy coming into form and form reverting to energy in the unending continuity of life.

BROWN BEAR MEDICINE

YOUR IN-DEPTH PERSONALITY PROFILE

SEASON OF BIRTH
HARVESTING TIME

THE FRUITFULNESS OF SUMMER IS ENJOYED DURING THE
THIRD BIRTH TIME OF THE SEASON, LENDING THOSE BORN
THEN THE QUALITIES OF GENEROSITY AND DILIGENCE.

H arvesting time is one of the twelve birth times, the fundamental division of the year into twelve seasonal segments (see pp.12–13). As the third period of the Summer cycle, it is the time of year when the Sun's energy is waning and the days are shortening as Autumn approaches. It is a time for reaping the produce of the plants sown in the Spring.

INFLUENCE OF NATURE
The qualities and characteristics imbued in Nature at this time form the basis of your own nature. So, just

as Nature is providing the fruits of the seeds sown in the Spring, so, if you were born during Harvesting time, you are both generous to others and concerned with reaping the rewards of your own efforts. You recognize that the quality of the harvest is largely dependent on how well the plants are tended as they grow. Accordingly, you invest much energy in discovering your talents and honing your skills in an effort to fulfill your potential. You believe we gain from life in proportion to the contribution made through practical endeavor.

As the nights draw in, this is a period that emphasizes the importance of painstakingly gathering what is of material value from that which is close at hand, in readiness for the Autumn and Winter. In a similar way, you appreciate the value of material things and tend to gain security by surrounding yourself with them.

STAGE OF LIFE

This time of year might be compared to the time of life when adulthood reaches maturity. In human development terms, it is a period of self-analysis and hard work. It is a time when practical skills are developed and fine-tuned, and the knowledge gained from experiences of childhood and early adulthood is evaluated. This is a period when life is approached with greater caution and patience than before.

ACHIEVE YOUR POTENTIAL

Your careful nature and affinity with the Earth means that you thrive best in a familiar environment in which you have already established your roots and position. You are extremely

Nature's energy

Nature offers the fruits of the Earth's labors in this, the last cycle of Summer before the Autumn equinox. Most wild berries are ready for gathering, and the crops have ripened and can now be harvested.

conscientious and reliable, with a remarkable consideration for the well-being of others. This means that you are generally regarded as a loyal and dependable friend.

Try not to allow your anxiety over the new or untested to prevent you from breaking the mold occasionally. Too much careful analysis of a situation or problem can sometimes create even more confusion. Learn to trust your instincts and feelings as well as your reason.

"Life is a circle from childhood to childhood; so it is with everything where power moves." Black Elk teaching

BIRTH TOTEM
THE BROWN BEAR

THE ESSENTIAL NATURE AND CHARACTERISTIC BEHAVIOR
OF THE BROWN BEAR EXPRESSES THE PERSONALITY TYPE
OF THOSE BORN DURING HARVESTING TIME.

Like the brown bear, people born during Harvesting time are resourceful and good-natured. If you were born at this time, you have an independent, considerate, painstaking, and modest nature that thrives in a secure, orderly environment.

Self-reliant and meticulous, you are conscientious and caring in your approach to work and relationships. Your enjoyment of routine and love of the familiar makes you loyal, dependable, and hard-working. It also means that you are reluctant to accept or effect changes in your life.

Constructive and practical, with an eye for detail, you have a talent for analysis that enables you to break down large tasks or problems into more manageable portions. Try to ensure that any focus on detail does not result in your losing sight of the overall picture.

Modest and generous toward others, you tend to minimize your own abilities and potential. As a result, you usually underestimate the quality or usefulness of your ideas and often fail to convert your dreams and aspirations into reality. In addition, your talents sometimes go unrecognized by others who tend to take advantage of your good nature. Sing your own praises more and refuse to take on more than you can comfortably manage in order to meet the expectations of others.

HEALTH MATTERS

Because of your love of practical work and crafts, your hands and feet are especially vulnerable to injury. Anxiety caused by threats to your security or the inability to express your true feelings can also make you prone to discomfort from an upset stomach, problems with the bowels, or skin disorders.

Brown Bear power

The brown bear expresses the strong and resourceful aspects of the modest, caring, and reliable people born at this time.

THE BROWN BEAR AND
RELATIONSHIPS

CARING AND DEPENDABLE, BROWN BEAR PEOPLE ARE
HIGHLY VALUED AS FRIENDS. THEY MAKE WARM AND
LOYAL PARTNERS BUT TEND TO HIDE THEIR FEELINGS.

Resourceful and good-natured, Brown Bear people, like their totem animal, are self-reliant and like to show their independence. If your birth totem is Brown Bear, you are considerate and conscientious, a good friend and colleague. Your constructive nature means you enjoy healing discord, so you often help mend tensions between those around you. You dislike imposing on others and may appear cold, which may lead to periods of loneliness.

LOVING RELATIONSHIPS
Brown Bear people make devoted and caring partners but may take a long time to establish a relationship. Both males and females are generous and reasonable but fond of routine and averse to change. Brown Bears

are usually gentle and tender lovers, considerate of a partner's needs.

When problems in relationships arise, it is often because you find it hard to express your emotions. You are uncomfortable with deep feelings so may seem cold and aloof at times, which leads to upsets and misunderstandings. Your dislike of change can also be frustrating.

COPING WITH BROWN BEAR
Brown Bear people hate uncertainty, so always let them know where they stand. Help them to ground their original ideas and creative schemes in practical ways, and you will forge a strong bond between you. Beware of showing strong emotions too quickly or they will take flight. Be gentle and proceed slowly if you want to win their affection and trust.

BROWN BEAR IN LOVE

Brown Bear with Falcon
Brown Bear's stability may not accord with Falcon's impetuosity, but this can be an invigorating partnership.

Brown Bear with Beaver
They may take time to warm to one another, but they should get along fine since they have a similar outlook.

Brown Bear with Deer This match might flounder after the initial spark, but Deer's lively manner may help Brown Bear have more fun.

Brown Bear with Woodpecker Both can be nurturing and sensitive to each other's needs, so they can form a good partnership.

Brown Bear with Salmon
Despite their incompatible outlooks, these two can make their differences work due to their warm natures.

Brown Bear with Brown Bear Brown Bears can have a long-lasting partnership if they encourage each other

to overcome timidity and express their true feelings.

Brown Bear with Crow A good-natured pairing, for both are easygoing and fair-minded. They may need to work to keep passion alive.

Brown Bear with Snake
They enjoy being together, but Snake may be too intense for Brown Bear.

Brown Bear with Owl A stable partnership, which may be full of surprises but perhaps lacking in passion.

Brown Bear with Goose
This relationship is bonded not so much sexually but by commitment and sharing.

Brown Bear with Otter
They have much in common and can form a lasting team, but may suffer conflicts. Their love life may lack spice.

Brown Bear with Wolf A mutually fulfilling and harmonious match, for each is naturally sensitive with a great capacity for love.

DIRECTIONAL TOTEM
THE MOUSE

THE MOUSE SYMBOLIZES THE INFLUENCE OF THE SOUTH ON BROWN BEAR PEOPLE, WHO CAN GAIN GREATER FULFILLMENT BY TUNING INTO THEIR EMOTIONS.

L ong Days time, Ripening time, and Harvesting time all fall within the quarter of the Medicine Wheel associated with the South Direction or Wind. The South is aligned with Summer and the bright warmth of midday, and it is associated with trust and innocence, depth of feeling, a sense of wonder, and hope. The power of the South's influence is primarily with the emotions, and its principal function is the power of giving. It takes as its totem the sensitive, curious, easily overlooked mouse.

The specific influence of the South on Brown Bear people is on emotional understanding, suffusing practical endeavors with desire and

Warrior mouse doll
This Hopi Kachina doll represents the mouse, which is associated with emotional sensitivity.

feeling so that they yield the full fruit of their rich potential. There is also an emphasis on allowing your spiritual and intuitive energies to develop, bringing about an expansion of awareness that is beyond the physical.

MOUSE CHARACTERISTICS
The mouse has whiskers that make it particularly sensitive to its surroundings through touch, so Native Americans believed it symbolized the power of perception

through closeness to things and through feelings. Its tiny size means it may be disregarded – just as we often overlook the small, true voice of our inner self. It also expresses curiosity, the value of experiencing through exploration and involvement, and a capacity to learn and develop at considerable speed.

The spirit of the South

The Sun is at its zenith in the South, symbolizing joy in life; the Mouse totem signifies heightened perception.

If your Directional totem is Mouse, you are likely to be highly sensitive to atmosphere and to the moods of those around you. You need to pay greater attention to your emotions, which you have the power to balance with your innate wisdom and good sense. Your keen eye for detail fuels your ability to learn and make rapid development, and you know that great achievements may grow from small beginnings.

ELEMENTAL TOTEM
THE TURTLE

LIKE THE TURTLE, WHICH PROCEEDS WITH PATIENT
TENACITY, DREAMY BROWN BEAR PEOPLE ACHIEVE MOST
WHEN THEY TAKE LIFE ONE STEP AT A TIME.

T he Elemental Aspect of
Brown Bear people is
Earth. They share this
Aspect with Beaver and Goose
people, who all therefore belong to
the same Elemental family or "clan"
(see pp.20–21 for an introduction to
the influence of the Elements).

THE TURTLE CLAN
Each Elemental clan has a totem
to provide insight into its essential
characteristics. The totem of the
Elemental clan of Earth is Turtle,
which symbolizes durability with a
careful, persistent, practical, and
methodical nature.

Down to Earth
*The turtle symbolizes the fundamental
qualities of the Element of Earth:
stability and the capacity for persistence.*

The turtle is a gentle creature, working steadily toward its desired destination at its own pace. So, if you belong to this clan, you will have a patient, down-to-earth personality, tenacious in pursuit of your goals.

Constructive and creative, you are happy to work hard to overcome obstacles and get results. You dislike disorder and tend to feel threatened by change. You can be inflexible and stubborn, and crave stability in order to feel at ease.

ELEMENTAL PROFILE

For Brown Bear people, the predominant Elemental Aspect of durable Earth is fundamentally affected by the qualities of your Principal Element – emotional Water. If you were born at this time, you are likely to be both highly practical and strongly creative; your earthly endeavors and projects draw power from your vivid imagination and deep feelings.

Earth of Water
The Element of Earth feeds Water, generating practicality coupled with imagination.

You may tend to lose sight of your true priorities and become bogged down in detail, driven by the emotional flux of Water and the urge for stability inherent in Earth. So you may sometimes find yourself in situations where you feel stuck or have problems expressing your needs and emotions clearly.

At times like these, or when you are feeling low or lacking in energy, try the following revitalizing exercise. Find a quiet spot in a garden, park, or woodland, away from traffic fumes and the activities of others.

You have an instinctive affinity for the Earth and plants, so sit or stand with both feet firmly in contact with the ground, and simply receive the natural beauty around you. Allow the energizing power of the life force to refresh your body, mind, and spirit.

STONE AFFINITY
TOPAZ

By using the gemstone with which your own
essence resonates, you can tap into the power of
the Earth itself and awaken your inner strengths.

Gemstones are minerals that are formed within the Earth itself in an exceedingly slow but continuous process. Native Americans valued gemstones not only for their beauty but also for being literally part of the Earth, and therefore possessing part of its life force. They regarded gemstones as being "alive" – channelers of energy that could be used in many ways: to heal, to protect, or for meditation.

Every gemstone has a different energy or vibration. On the Medicine Wheel, a stone is associated with each birth time, the energy of which resonates with the essence of those

Faceted topaz

Native Americans likened the color of golden topaz to the glow of the Sun at the dawn of a new day.

born during that time. Because of this energy affiliation, your gemstone can be used to help bring you into harmony with the Earth and to create balance within yourself. It can enhance and develop your good qualities and endow you with the qualities or abilities you need.

ENERGY RESONANCE

Brown Bear people have an affinity with topaz, which occurs in a range of colors – golden yellow and pink are the most valuable. Topaz is sometimes referred to as "the stone of success" because it is thought to attract positive energies that help

ACTIVATE YOUR GEMSTONE

O btain either a rough or polished topaz and cleanse it by holding it under cold running water. Allow it to dry naturally. Then, holding the stone with both hands, bring it up to your mouth and blow into it sharply and hard, three or four times in order to impregnate it with your breath. Next, hold it firmly in one hand, and silently welcome it into your life as a friend and helper.

When you are faced with a problem or are feeling unclear, use the topaz to help you meditate on the issue. Find a quiet spot to sit without fear of interruption, and place the topaz in front of you. Focus on it, keeping its image in mind even if you let your eyes close, and allow it to bring you clarity. Listen for the still, small voice of your inner self.

transform thoughts and ideas into action. Native Americans regarded it as a stone of hope,. They used it in an elixir to heal various disorders and skin problems. It is also reputed to dispel anxiety.

If your birth totem is Brown Bear, you will find topaz especially useful in helping you to express your ideas clearly. It is believed to dissipate feelings of restriction and to enable you to recognize promising new

Topaz power
Carry a topaz with you in a pouch or keep it in your living room – its vibrations can promote confidence.

opportunities. Topaz enhances your ability to be focused and increases the likelihood of your achieving the results your talents merit, making it valuable to Brown Bear people, who tend to underestimate their abilities.

"The outline of the stone is round; the power of the stone is endless." *Lakota Sioux teaching*

TREE AFFINITY
HORNBEAM

GAIN A DEEPER UNDERSTANDING OF YOUR OWN NATURE
AND AWAKEN POWERS LYING DORMANT WITHIN YOU BY
RESPECTING AND CONNECTING WITH YOUR AFFINITY TREE.

Trees have an important part to play in the protection of Nature's mechanisms and in the maintenance of the Earth's atmospheric balance, which is essential for the survival of the human race.

Native Americans referred to trees as "Standing People" because they stand firm, obtaining strength from their connection with the Earth. They therefore teach us the importance of being grounded, while at the same time listening to and reaching for our higher aspirations. When respected as living beings, trees can provide insight into the workings of Nature and our own inner selves.

On the Medicine Wheel, each birth time is associated with a particular kind of tree, the basic qualities of which complement the nature of those born during that time. Brown Bear people have an affinity with the hornbeam. Called "the great provider," the hornbeam releases its winged seeds into the wind like a parent sending offspring out into the world. This sturdy tree is

CONNECT WITH YOUR TREE

Appreciate the beauty of your affinity tree and study its nature carefully, for it has an affinity with your own nature.

The hornbeam is a beechlike tree with fresh green leaves that turn yellow and orange in Autumn. In Spring, it bears both yellow and green catkins, and in Autumn, it produces nuts with papery wings that carry the seed in the wind.

Try the following exercise when you need to revitalize your inner strength. Stand beside your affinity tree. Place the palms of your hands on its trunk and rest your forehead on the backs of your hands. Inhale slowly and feel energy from the tree's roots flow through your body. If easily available, obtain a cutting or twig from your affinity tree to keep as a totem or helper.

highly valued as a windbreak, offering shelter to less resilient companions, while its canopy lets in beams of uplifting sunlight. When practical concerns weigh heavily, Brown Bear people can renew their powers of inspiration by connecting with their tree (see panel above).

LEARNING TO LET GO

If your birth totem is Brown Bear, you are dependable, practical, and considerate, although you tend to undervalue your own talents. Your need for security and comfort can lead you to become bogged down by practical details and constrained because you avoid unknown paths.

Like the hornbeam releasing its seeds, learn to let go and trust your instincts a little more; you will open up opportunities to develop your potential and enjoy the many gifts you have to offer. Call on the hornbeam for its inspirational energy to help you find greater freedom.

*"All healing plants are given by Wakan-Tanka;
therefore they are holy."* Lakota Sioux teaching

COLOR AFFINITY
BROWN

Enhance your positive qualities by using the power of your affinity color to affect your emotional and mental states.

Each birth time has an affinity with a particular color. This is the color that resonates best with the energies of the people born during that time. Exposure to your affinity color will encourage a positive emotional and mental outlook, while exposure to colors that clash with your affinity color will have a negative effect on your entire sense of well-being.

Brown resonates with Brown Bear people. Made up of equal parts orange and violet, it combines the influence of both these colors. Orange is associated with energy, enthusiasm, and ambition, and violet with power and spiritual values; mixed as brown, they combine to suggest integrity, security, and dependability. It is a supportive color that signals conscientiousness,

Color scheme
Let a brown or tan color theme be the thread that runs through your home, from the furnishings and fixtures to the walls and floors.

MEDITATE ON YOUR COLOR

Find a small wooden object – a bowl, vase, ornament, or carving. Take it to a room in which you will not be disturbed for at least half an hour, and place it on a table.

Sit at the table, face the object, and focus all your attention on it. Relax your body and concentrate your mind solely on the color. Sense the texture of the color, and experience the feelings of stability and security it emits. Now bring to mind a specific goal that you wish to achieve or a particular problem that you wish to overcome. Allow any thoughts and sensations to flow throughout your mind and body: experience and reflect on them as they happen.

loyalty, and a methodical approach to life, peppered with occasional flights of fancy. Brown also suggests a commitment to establishing firm foundations from which to develop long-term objectives.

COLOR BENEFITS

Strengthen your aura and enhance your positive qualities by introducing shades of brown – tan, chocolate, fawn – to the interior decor of your home. Spots of color can make all the difference. Curtains containing brown patterning, for example, can alter the ambience of a room, or try displaying an arrangement of dried flowers in a bronze or copper vase.

If you need a confidence boost, wear something that contains brown. Whenever your energies are low, practice the color meditation exercise outlined above to balance your emotions, awaken your creativity, and help you to feel joyful.

"The power of the spirit should be honored with its color." Lakota Sioux teaching

WORKING THE WHEEL
LIFE PATH

CONSIDER YOUR BIRTH PROFILE AS A STARTING POINT IN
THE DEVELOPMENT OF YOUR CHARACTER AND THE
ACHIEVEMENT OF PERSONAL FULFILLMENT.

Each of the twelve birth times is associated with a particular path of learning or with a collection of lessons to be learned through life. By following your path of learning, you will develop strengths in place of weaknesses, achieve a greater sense of harmony with the world, and discover inner peace.

YOUR PATH OF LEARNING
For Brown Bear people, the first lesson on your path of learning is to develop the

ability to convert your dreams and aspirations into reality. You are an original thinker with a vivid imagination. However, many of your ideas are never developed because you fail either to appreciate their true value or to understand how to apply them to your life. Next time you have an idea, treat it with respect; analyze it fully and consider the variety of ways it could be

"Each man's road is shown to him within his own heart. There he sees all the truths of life." Cheyenne teaching

implemented. By grounding your dreams, you are far more likely to incorporate them into your life.

Brown Bear people must also learn when it is appropriate to make alterations in their lives. You are very much a creature of habit, disliking change and preferring the familiar to the new. This can mean that you persist with routines or patterns of behavior long after they have outgrown their usefulness. Try to evaluate your level of satisfaction in the key areas of your life, and consider whether some changes might be beneficial.

Your third lesson is to learn not to fear the strength of your feelings. When your feelings well up inside, you tend to hide them beneath a mask of casualness. Such behavior can make you appear cool and aloof, and often results in upsetting and needless misunderstandings. Try to overcome your fear, and find ways of expressing your true feelings.

WORKING THE WHEEL
MEDICINE POWER

HARNESS THE POWERS OF OTHER BIRTH TIMES TO
TRANSFORM YOUR WEAKNESSES INTO STRENGTHS AND
TO MEET THE CHALLENGES IN YOUR LIFE.

The whole spectrum of human qualities and abilities is represented on the Medicine Wheel. The totems and affinities associated with each birth time indicate the basic qualities with which those born at that time are equipped.

Complementary affinity
*A key strength of Wolf – weak in
Brown Bear – is the ability to
perceive the whole.*

Study your path of learning (see pp.42–43) to identify those aspects of your personality that may need to be strengthened, then look at other birth times to discover the totems and affinities that can assist you in this task. For example, your Elemental profile is Earth of Water (see pp.34–35), so for balance you need the freedom and clarity of Air

and the enthusiasm of Fire. Deer's Elemental profile is Air of Fire and Falcon's is Fire of Fire, so meditate on these birth totems. In addition, you may find it useful to study the profiles of the other two members of your Elemental clan of Turtle – Beaver and Goose – to discover how the same Elemental Aspect of Earth can be expressed differently.

Also helpful is the birth totem that sits opposite yours on the Medicine Wheel, which usually contains qualities that complement or enhance your own. This is known as your complementary affinity, which for Brown Bear people is Wolf.

ESSENTIAL STRENGTHS

Described below are the essential strengths of each birth totem. To develop a quality that is weak in yourself or that you need to meet a particular challenge, meditate upon the birth totem that contains the attribute you need. Obtain a representation of the relevant totem – a claw, tooth, or feather; a picture, ring, or model. Affirm that the power it represents is within you.

Falcon medicine is the power of keen observation and the ability to act decisively and energetically whenever action is required..

Beaver medicine is the ability to think creatively and laterally – to develop alternative ways of doing or thinking about things.

Deer medicine is characterized by sensitivity to the intentions of others and to that which might be detrimental to your well-being.

Woodpecker medicine is the ability to establish a steady rhythm throughout life and to be tenacious in protecting all that you value.

Salmon medicine is the strength to be determined and courageous in the choice of goals you want to achieve and to have enough stamina to see a task through to the end.

Brown Bear medicine is the ability to be resourceful, hardworking, and dependable in times of need, and to draw on inner strength.

Crow medicine is the ability to transform negative or nonproductive situations into positive ones and to transcend limitations.

Snake medicine is the talent to adapt easily to changes in circumstances and to manage transitional phases well.

Owl medicine is the power to see clearly during times of uncertainty and to conduct life consistently, according to long-term plans.

Goose medicine is the courage to do whatever might be necessary to protect your ideals and to adhere to your principles in life.

Otter medicine is the ability to connect with your inner child, to be innovative and idealistic, and to thoroughly enjoy the ordinary tasks and routines of everyday life.

Wolf medicine is the courage to act according to your intuition and instincts rather than your intellect, and to be compassionate.